WORKBOOK

FOR

BURNOUT

The Secret to Unlocking the Stress Cycle

THIS BOOK BELONGS TO

_____

_____

HOW TO USE THIS WORKBOOK FOR YOUR MAXIMUM BENEFIT

Are you ready to positively transform and turn your life around?

Then come along on this journey of personal development as you provoke your thought and get deeper insight into the original book.

Stretch your limits, surpass your boundaries, leave your comfort zone and achieve the impossible as you work your way through this book.

This book is a companion book to *"Burnout: The Secret to Unlocking the Stress Cycle by Emily Nagoski PhD, Amelia Nagoski DMA"*.

Each section of the original book has been comprehensively covered and broken down giving you more perspective with thought-provoking questions, goals, key takeaways/talking points, lessons, self-reflections, action plans, notes and a lot more.

When dealing with the questions in each section, take your time and think over them and be sincere and truthful with each answer.

Remember, this is a **safe space,** for you to freely express yourself without being judged.

In addition, put everything from this book into practice in your real life to see all-round improvements.

It is time to discover and rediscover yourself.

INTRODUCTION

Have you ever felt overwhelmed and exhausted with all the things you have to do and still wonder if you are doing "enough"? Then this book is just what you need.

As you go through life, you have probably tried all the advices you have heard to make you feel more relaxed. Such advices must have included at least one of the following; exercise, self-compassion, mindfulness, coloring books, bubble baths, gratitude and whole lot of others.

Just like you, other women around the world have tried same with little or no success in finding the balance between giving adequate attention to their kids, partners, jobs and other areas of their lives.

As a woman, you are constantly trying to give your best and your failure is not for the lack of trying.

One problem in our world today is that "wellness" has been turned into something that we must all strive for, but only the rich and wealthy that can actually achieve it.

With this book, you can now figure out how to make wellness be like your actual real life and every barrier standing between you and your well-being would be confronted and brought down.

Set a positive goal for yourself, because as humans, we tend to thrive better when we have something positive to move toward.

It doesn't matter where you are in life, whether you are currently battling in the pit of hopelessness and looking for an exit, or if your life is fantastic and you just want something to make it greater, you would discover some hidden gems in these pages.

And now with this book, you would understand how best to unlock the stress cycle and overcome burnout.

Some other vital life lessons you would learn are;

- How to effectively complete the biological stress cycle
- Managing the "monitor" in your brain to help you regulate the emotion of frustration
- How to defend yourself against the Bikini Industrial Complex
- How to befriend your inner critic.
- Recovering from burnout and preventing it through rest and human connection
- And a so much more

PART ONE: WHAT YOU TAKE WITH YOU

CHAPTER ONE: COMPLETE THE CYCLE

KEY TAKEAWAYS & CRUCIAL POINTS

➢ Stress responses in our bodies are activated by stressors and they can either be external or internal stressors which your body can interpret as potential threats.

➢ External stressors (money, work, cultural norms, family, expectations, etc.) are more tangible than internal stressors (self-criticism, identity, memories, worries about the future, body image, etc.).

➢ Stress can cause a change in your mind or entire body due to the neurological and physiological shift that occurs.

➢ Eliminating the stressor (cause of the stress) is not enough to complete the stress response cycle since your body would still remain in full action mode and not relaxed.

➢ A feeling of helplessness and emotional exhaustion are both ever-present when someone experiences burnout.

➢ Some other strategies of completing the stress cycle are deep, slow breathing, positive social interaction, laughter, affection or deep connection with a loving presence, crying and creative expression.

SESSION ONE

In what ways did your upbringing affect the way you handle uncomfortable emotions and situations?

(blank lined response area)

List those stress-activating situations around you in your day-to-day life and write one way you think you can avoid them.

(blank lined response area)

Use the space below to plan out your creative activities for the next few days.

Do you think allowing yourself to feel stress and other uncomfortable emotions, is wrong and makes you appear weak?

In the past, how do you deal with your stress?

My Personal Reflection

_____
_____
_____
_____
_____
_____
_____

Lessons Learnt from Chapter   I Seek improvement in...

_____   _____
_____   _____
_____   _____
_____   _____
_____   _____
_____   _____

How This Chapter Made me feel

_____
_____
_____
_____
_____
_____
_____
_____

———————

I Am Grateful for...	My Top 3 Goals
_____	_____
_____	_____
_____	_____
_____	_____

MY DAILY ACTION PLAN

Sunday

Monday

Tuesday

Wednesday

Thursday

Friday

Saturday

CHAPTER 2: #PERSIST

KEY TAKEAWAYS & CRUCIAL POINTS

> It is important to adequately manage the stressors and know how to persist or quit when you're past the edge of your individual capabilities.

> In the brain, the mechanism that helps manage the gap between where we are and where we are going, is called the Monitor and it is this is also responsible for deciding if we keep on trying or just give up.

> When you put in less effort and achieve great results or progress, your Monitor is satisfied.

> A high effort or investment with little results or progress leads to a ragey Monitor.

> Understanding how the Monitor works gives us the ability to control or influence the functioning of our brain and provides strategies to deal with stressors, whether the controllable ones or the uncontrollable ones.

> Positive reappraisal can reduce stress and increase your creativity and capacity to cope with greater difficulties in the future.

SESSION TWO

What is your frustrating goal?

Why do you feel that this particular goal frustrates your monitor?

How much does this goal matter to you?

Think of 20 options for definitions of 'winning'. Let these
definitions, satisfy your monitor.

Write out those goals you have been trying to each for some time now and next to each, rank your effort on a scale of 1 to 10; 10 being the highest possible effort, 5 would be average and 1 means you put in the least possible effort.

Are you someone that naturally notices the positives or something valuable from difficult situations?

What are your short and long-term benefits of keeping your goal?

What are your short and long-term benefits of letting go of the goal?

Recall any difficult moment in your life you were able to find opportunities in.

My Personal Reflection

_____

_____

_____

_____

_____

_____

_____

—————————————

Lessons Learnt from Chapter

_____

_____

_____

_____

I Seek improvement in...

_____

_____

_____

_____

How This Chapter Made me feel

_____

_____

_____

_____

_____

_____

_____

_____

————————

I Am Grateful for...

_____

_____

_____

_____

My Top 3 Goals

_____

_____

_____

MY DAILY ACTION PLAN

Sunday

Monday

Tuesday

Wednesday

Thursday

Friday

Saturday

CHAPTER 3: MEANING

KEY TAKEAWAYS & CRUCIAL POINTS

➤ The power of meaning lies in its ability to make us know why something is happening, and this makes it easier to accept.

➤ With the power of "meaning" which you carry inside you, you can resist and recover from burnout.

➤ Using the approach of positive psychology, meaning is one of the elements that promotes happiness, while other research approaches see meaning as a strategy employed to cope with tough issues of life like illness or trauma.

➤ Human Giver Syndrome is a moral obligation to *give* your entire humanity and it can be looked at as a virus whose aim is to preserve its own existence.

SESSION THREE

Do you have any ambitious goal that has a potential to leave a legacy behind? Talk about it briefly in the space below.

| |
| |
| |
| |

Based on the tough situation you are going through at the moment, write out some tough questions you would like to know the answers to and reflect on each.

What is that "Something Larger" for you that gives you a
sense of calling?

| |
| |
| |
| |
| |
| |
| |

Ask your closest friend to describe the "real you", pointing
out the characteristics of your personality that are at the
core of your best self. Write down his/her answer.

| |
| |
| |
| |
| |
| |

My Personal Reflection

_____

_____

_____

_____

_____

_____

_____

_____

Lessons Learnt from Chapter	I Seek improvement in...
_____	_____
_____	_____
_____	_____
_____	_____
_____	_____

How This Chapter Made me feel

_____
_____
_____
_____
_____
_____
_____
_____

———————

I Am Grateful for...	My Top 3 Goals
_____	_____
_____	_____
_____	_____
_____	_____

MY DAILY ACTION PLAN

Sunday

Monday

Tuesday

Wednesday

Thursday

Friday

Saturday

PART II

THE REAL ENEMY

CHAPTER 4: THE GAME IS RIGGED

KEY TAKEAWAYS

➤ We all have the resources within us to complete our stress cycle, manage our Monitor and engage with our Something Larger.

➤ Completing our stress cycle, managing our Monitor and engaging with our Something Larger does not depend on our location or the culture we find ourselves in.

➤ Learned helplessness takes you straight past frustration and into the pit of despair, and this is not a rational choice.

➤ Our ability to see gender-based inequalities, injustice and imbalances as unfair can be limited by the Human Giver Syndrome which blinds our sensitivity to patriarchy (ugh).

➤ Gaslighting can make you question your own credibility and competence.

SESSION FOUR

How does the word "patriarchy" make you feel?

```
┌────────────────────────────────────────────────────────┐
│                                                        │
└────────────────────────────────────────────────────────┘
```

What do you do to engage your Something Larger and also smash some patriarchy?

Do you feel like your voice is being silenced in your office, school, home or around your community?

| |
| |

When you recognize it, how do you feel when someone is gaslighting you?

| |
| |
| |
| |
| |

What are the signs of compassion fatigue you notice in yourself?

| |
| |
| |
| |
| |

My Personal Reflection

_____
_____
_____
_____
_____
_____
_____
_____

———————

Lessons Learnt from Chapter

I Seek improvement in...

_____	_____
_____	_____
_____	_____
_____	_____
_____	_____

How This Chapter Made me feel

_____
_____
_____
_____
_____
_____
_____
_____

——————

I Am Grateful for...	My Top 3 Goals
_____	_____
_____	_____
_____	_____
_____	_____
_____	_____

MY DAILY ACTION PLAN

Sunday

Monday

Tuesday

Wednesday

Thursday

Friday

Saturday

CHAPTER 5: THE BIKINI INDUSTRIAL COMPLEX

KEY TAKEAWAYS & CRUCIAL POINTS

➤ No matter what has happened right from the day you were born until now, your body is still perfect and beautiful and full of needs.

➤ Culture is one reason why more and more women are engaging in weight-control behaviors.

➤ When you accept the lies about the relationship between weight and health, you constantly try to change your weight.

➤ Losing weight does not automatically mean you would live longer.

➤ Thin privilege is just as real in our society as race, class and gender.

SESSIONS FIVE

What are your thoughts of the prevalence of weight control behavior engaged by adolescents in our society today?

At what age did you start becoming worried about being "too fat"?

What advice can you give to someone who is risking her health or life in order to attain a particular beauty ideal?

My Personal Reflection

_____
_____
_____
_____
_____
_____
_____
_____

————————————

Lessons Learnt from Chapter

I Seek improvement in...

_____   _____

_____   _____

_____   _____

_____   _____

_____   _____

How This Chapter Made me feel

_____

_____

_____

_____

_____

_____

_____

_____

I Am Grateful for...	My Top 3 Goals
_____	_____
_____	_____
_____	_____
_____	_____

MY DAILY ACTION PLAN

Sunday

Monday

Tuesday

Wednesday

Thursday

Friday

Saturday

PART III

WAX ON, WAX OFF

CHAPTER 6: ROUTINE

KEY TAKEAWAYS

➢ Connection is a primary source of strength, just like any other basic biological need we have.

➢ Social connection can be seen as a form of nourishment and our experiences of connection help shape our present relationships with others.

➢ Even though our need for connection would change across our life spans, but our basic fundamental need for connection doesn't change.

➢ When we exchange loving looks, example between a mother and child, dopamine is released. This neuropeptide is what bonds us with others and facilitates the growth of neuropeptide connections.

➢ The exchange of negative looks releases cortisol which is a stress hormone that hinders the production of neural connections.

SESSION SIX

What effect (positive or negative) has been felt in your current relationship as a result of your earlier social interaction.

Discuss the nourishing effect you feel as a result of connection.

Before reading the main book, what has been your own definition of trust?

What are the positive relationships you have in your life?

My Personal Reflection

_____

_____

_____

_____

_____

_____

_____

_____

_____

Lessons Learnt from Chapter	I Seek improvement in...
_____	_____
_____	_____
_____	_____
_____	_____
_____	_____

How This Chapter Made me feel

_____
_____
_____
_____
_____
_____
_____
_____

_____

I Am Grateful for...	My Top 3 Goals
_____	_____
_____	_____
_____	_____
_____	_____

MY DAILY ACTION PLAN

Sunday

Monday

Tuesday

Wednesday

Thursday

Friday

Saturday

CHAPTER 7: WHAT MAKES YOU STRONGER

KEY TAKEAWAYS

➤ It is incorrect to feel that you can employ "grit" or "self-control" to keep yourself focused and productive every moment of each day. This is also gaslighting and has the potential to damage your brain.

➤ Even though sleeping is necessary for our survival, we find ourselves criticizing ourselves and feeling guilty for sleeping. This is as a result of the barrier put between us and rest due to the Human Giver Syndrome

➤ Since rest is what makes you stronger and the Human Giver Syndrome doesn't want you to rest, we can safely say that the Human Giver Syndrome doesn't want you to be strong, joyful, healthy and confident.

➤ Apart from making you productive, rest also makes you happier, more creative, less grumpy and a lot healthier.

SESSION SEVEN

What are the regularly occurring events in your life that limit you from having enough rest. Write them down and see if you can block some of them.

How would you handle a situation where someone unloads his/her stress on you?

Do not believe other people's opinions about your body but only believe what your body is telling you. What are those opinions you have believed?

My Personal Reflection

_____

Lessons Learnt from Chapter

I Seek improvement in...

How This Chapter Made me feel

_____
_____
_____
_____
_____
_____
_____

―――――――――――

I Am Grateful for...	My Top 3 Goals

MY DAILY ACTION PLAN

Sunday

Monday

Tuesday

Wednesday

Thursday

Friday

Saturday

CHAPTER 8: GROW MIGHTY

KEY TAKEAWAYS

- ➢ Wellness is a state of action and not a state of mind; an ongoing mutual exchange of support where givers give and also accept support.
- ➢ Living joyfully ever after comes from the connection with other givers just like you.
- ➢ Become aware that you deserve respect, kindness and to be cherished and loved.

SESSION EIGHT

Get to know your "madwoman" now as you describe her in the space below.

Write her feelings and thoughts and what she says to you?
Take note of those areas where she criticizes you harshly
and know that these are sources of exhaustion.

Thank her for all the hard work done in order to help you
survive.

My Personal Reflection

_____
_____
_____
_____
_____
_____
_____
_____

━━━━━━━━━━━━━━━━━━

Lessons Learnt from Chapter   I Seek improvement in...

_____   _____

_____   _____

_____   _____

_____   _____

_____   _____

How This Chapter Made me feel

_____
_____
_____
_____
_____
_____
_____
_____

I Am Grateful for...	My Top 3 Goals
_____	_____
_____	_____
_____	_____
_____	_____

MY DAILY ACTION PLAN

Sunday

Monday

Tuesday

Wednesday

Thursday

Friday

Saturday

NOTES